Inspire

To

Empower

Inspire
to
Empower

Table Of Contents

Foreword

In order to be able to complete a task satisfactorily takes a certain amount of motivation. Besides having the necessary skill and knowledge about the said task this element of motivation is what is going to keep the individual on track.

Motivate To Empower

Get Motivated And Inspired To Boost Your Energy Levels And Achieve Results Fast

Chapter 1:

What Does It Mean To Be Motivated

Synopsis

Self motivation is probable the single most important element in keeping an individual interested and committed to finishing a set task.

The doubt factor that is always present in every scenario requires some level of motivation in order to ensure the doubt is kept in check or at bay. In life it is not always possible to only do things or be exposed to things that only bring pleasure.

There will be times when some discipline is required to get through a task even if it is uncomfortable and displeasure able, and here is where one needs to be self motivated.

The Basics

Some of the things that may help an individual to stay motivated are as follows:

- Keeping the end goal in clear focus. When the end goal is clearly imprinted in the mind's eye, then the body and mind will be able to subconsciously condition themselves to suit the needs of the individual to successfully complete the task set.
- Continuously reminding one's self of the capabilities and the conviction that it is possible to finish the task. This continual reminder will then translate into a zest and even the chemical reaction within the body and mind that produces the extra energy to keep going.
- Stepping back and viewing the task in its present percentage of accomplishment will also help to create a further motivational level to complete it. This is more so when the physical accomplishment to that point is on the positive side.
- Facilitating little rewards to be enjoyed as each level in the task is achieved can also be a good motivational tool.

Chapter 2:

Synopsis

Most people just try to get through each day without really learning to appreciate it for all it has to offer. More so in todays fast pace world there is really very little opportunity to stop and think let alone indulge in something that may really be enjoyable to pursue. There is always the thought that "I will do it someday." Sometime however there is a need to stop and take stock of one's life to ensure the zest for living is still very much alive and well.

Important Info

In the process of taking a clear and serious look at one's life to date, several different questions should be asked and addressed in order to help the individual lead a more fruitful and motivated daily life. In pursing this, the individual will then be able to find happiness and contentment as the motivation levels will be higher than ever.

Having a goal in life that is both rewarding and achievable in the eye of the individual is what is going to keep the said individual on track and in success. Doing something that really brings joy and peace should not really be considered a privilege as it is possible to work towards finding something that brings on these positive feelings with a little focused understanding of one's self.

When this is clearly understood, the mind and the body will work together to make the circumstances possible to achieve anything desired. The inspiration needed to carry the mind set to completing the task will be the dominating factor.

Being able to identify what area of activities most benefits and excites the individual is also another advantage worth exploring. When one is excited about something there is very little need to push it to success.

Chapter 3:

Synopsis

Positive people are not only a joy to be around but they are also the people that get things done. Mostly they get whatever they work towards because of the motivation they utilize in order to always look at things from a positive mind set.

Altering Thinking

There are several ways to keep the negative elements or mind set away and from possibly causing problems from within. Here are some thoughts on the matter:

• Always try to stay calm in every situation. Panic does not help and can even cause irrevocable changes.

• Forcing one's self to keep a gentle tone will in turn force the body chemical to react better to the situation and thus work towards causing the mind to slowly calm down and relax.

• Always make it a habit to look for as many positive elements as possible in any given negative situation. When one constantly trains to look for the positive, the chances of letting the situation overwhelm and cause other negative vibes can be controlled successfully.

• Being around people who are equally positive will always prove to be a wise choice indeed. Positive people focus on staying positive no matter what the situation is, as opposed to being only able to stir up negative points.

• Coming to the realization that constantly taking the negative stand will only bring deeper and larger problems should be enough of a reason to start being positive.

• Learning from mistakes is sometimes the best way to move forward. This gives the individual a chance to exercise skills perhaps unknown or buried deep within. It can also be very satisfying when the negative is turned into a positive.

•   Listening to positive motivational messages and talking to people who advocate a constant positive mindset is also encouraged. The tips they impart can be invaluable.

Chapter 4:

Associate With Positive People

Synopsis

As previously mentioned there are a lot of merits in ensuring a positive mindset. Therefore going a step further and making the conscious effort to surround one's self with positive people always will in fact be the best formula to follow.

Positive

If an individual is seriously interested in becoming a better person, the first wise step to make is to ensure those within the inner circle in their lives or those in constant contact with them are always of the positive nature.

The general wisdom behind this thinking is that whatever positive practices and value held by these positive minded associates will eventually be copied and practiced by the individual too.

Negative people always find reasons to drag themselves and those around them down. Perhaps it is because they are more comfortable if everyone else is miserable too.

However positive people will take the time and effort to impart or impact as many positive values as they can to someone who is interested in achieving the same positive outlook in life as them.

Among the positive characteristics of positive people are the ability to be enthusiastic about almost anything, an uncanny zest for life, a willingness to try anything, cheerful, inspired are just a few to name. All these character traits are very enticing to be a part of and if an individual is open to being led then it is possible to learn to look at things through the eyes of these positive people and thus really begin to enjoy life.

Associating with positive people whenever the opportunity presents itself is also beneficial intellectually and in building stronger character traits. Positive people tend to be well informed and in the know always. They usually make a conscious effort to keep up with the latest in everything.

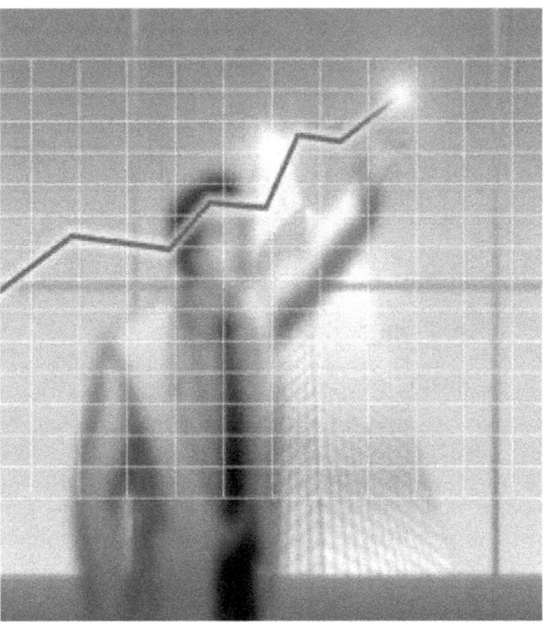

Chapter 5:

Put Your Goal Where You Can See It

Synopsis

In order to see a task to completion and with the same motivational levels as at the beginning of the task, it would be prudent to have the goal expected to be derived from the task to be as visible as possible. This not only applies to having this goal firmly imprinted in the mind's eye but also should be physically visible as much as possible.

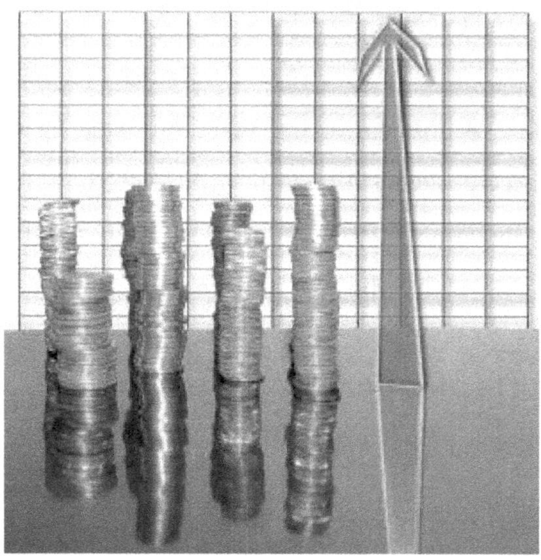

Look At It

If the goal is not only foremost in the thoughts of the individual but also "around" the individual than the battle to keep the task featured as a constant and important factor daily is achieved. Many people advocate the physical presence of the goal help to keep them focused until the end desired results are achieved.

Some of the ways that can be used successfully are putting up visual aids that depict the desired goal. Others may include keeping a log book of sorts to chart the progress made towards achieving the goal. There are some people that go as far as to have a replica of what they want to achieve made. The idea really is to keep the goal as visible as possible through any means available in order to keep the motivation levels as high and as constant as possible.

If the goal in question can be successfully broken up into different stages then keeping a chart that visibly tracks the progress of the task toward the end achievement, helps to create the necessary satisfaction levels within the individual in the visibility of the progress at hand. The nearer the end becomes visible the more the adrenaline levels will rise and thus produce more energy and zest to see the task perhaps achieved at a quicker pace. Getting friends to help keep track of the progress with the individual also helps to keep the goal in focus.

Chapter 6:

Reward Yourself For Small Advancements

Synopsis

Rewards are always a wonderful thing to receive especially if the efforts put into a task to achieve the rewards has been quite monumental. Rewards are also a great way to keep motivated and focus on the task to see it to completion.

Praise

Breaking a task into sections has many merits one of which is it allows the individual or those involved in the task process to be able to physically see the progress and monitor it accordingly.

This also creates the opportunity to pass out little rewards when each stage is achieved. These rewards are a great incentive to ensure those involved in the task are able to stay focus and totally committed to seeing the said task to successful completion.

However the types of rewards and the methods linked to meriting the rewards should be carefully considered lest it turn out to have adverse effects instead.

Drawing up a system that charts the progress and associates the different stages to different rewards given out should be done early on in the project frame work. The rewards chosen should match the progress made.

Choosing the right rewards is very important as it is supposed to act as an incentive and the wrong array of rewards may not cause those involved to be motivated but instead cause them to doubt their contribution values to the success of the project. This can indeed have very damaging result on the morale and general attitude towards keeping up the motivation to succeed.

Rewards that are tailored to bring on the excitement and satisfaction when a certain level in the project is reached will not only cause the added zest needed it will also contribute to the individual working harder to achieve the next level of advancement in order to be rewarded again. This new found added zest is very beneficial as these spurts of energy also bring new life into the project at every few stages.

Chapter 7:

Synopsis

Staying excited is a very important tool to ensure the mind set does not give up half way during the project started. This will not only be a bad habit to pick up it will also cause detrimental effects in the long run.

Energize

The excitement factor will always be able to motivate an individual to keep moving forward toward achieving the goals set. This key ingredient is what attracts people to consider or embark on a project. Those who stay excited have the positive mindset that is required and also necessary to ensure the success of any project or endeavor.

Sharing the ideas in the intended project with others helps to keep the excitement levels high. When a person is passionate about their endeavors it shows clearly in the way they talk about the project.

This excitement more often than not carries over to the others listening. There are even scientific researches done that attest to the proven facts that there are a lot of positive chemical changes that happen in the body system when the excitement levels are apparent.

Setting time lines and dates at every juncture of the project has its benefits is keeping the excitement levels high. Whenever these time lines or deal lines are successfully met the individual or group experiences another level of satisfaction which in turn creates the positive element of excitement.

Believing strongly in the project is also another way to keep being excited about the project. If the belief is strong then any and all negative encounters along the way can be easily overcome because of the excitement levels that can counter these setbacks that may occur from time to time. Most people who passionately believe in themselves and their abilities to successfully achieve anything are usually very well balanced and success orientated people.

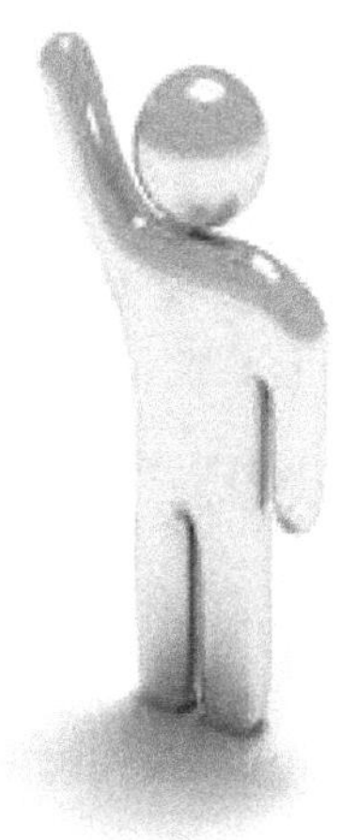

Chapter 8:

Learn To Be Dedicated

Synopsis

Dedication is also another prerequisite to being able to achieve many things impossible or otherwise. It is often one of the most important factors needed to be in place and evident even before a project is embarked upon.

Stay Focused

Some of the ways to stay as dedicated as possible are as follows:

• Having a love for what is required in terms of work processes in the project is important. Those people who tend to focus on the end goal rather than what it takes to get there, soon find out that they are in a rather unhappy and stressful journey. This then shifts the dedication commitment levels which can cause serious problems and effects to the project in question.

• Being dedicated is also being persistent. If the persistency element is evident then the individual is able to work hard and do whatever is required in order to complete any endeavor started.

• Keeping to a suitable and workable routine is also helpful as it shows the level of dedication involved. This not only helps the mind set but also allows the body to condition itself to work towards achieving the goal set.

• When the object of the goal brings a certain level of personal gratification and at the same time is also for the good of others the dedication levels an individual is prepared to extend can be phenomenal.

• Seeking help along the way may also show that the individual is very committed to completing the task. When faced with a problem that requires the expertise that the individual does not have, seeking outside help is one way of staying true to the project and maintaining the dedication levels.

- 25 -

• Being able to move forward when mistakes are made also requires a certain dedication level. The dedication levels evident will dictate the lengths the individual is willing to go in order to achieve success

Chapter 9:

Synopsis

Standing alone is never a good idea when trying to achieve something. Everyone needs friends and family to provide the necessary encouragement and help that is sometimes required to see any endeavor to its successful end.

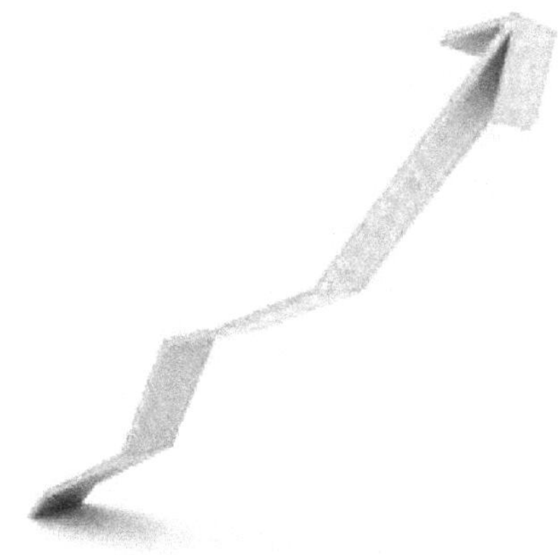

Some Suggestions

The support and encouragement from other can have very far reaching and powerful effects. These elements play a huge part in helping the individual keep up the zest, will or discipline to succeed.

Another reason it is important to have outside support is that sometime those not immediately connected to the project or endeavor can see more clearly the situation and make the helpful comments and give helpful advice. This is indeed invaluable to the individual who may be stuck in a rut and unable to see a way out.

Being open to accepting support can also create the circumstances for new relationships or opportunities to present itself. These can bring about a more fruitful and positive outcome and perhaps even a new positive light to the whole project. Closer ties can be fostered through the working together process which is facilitated by the support given.

Getting support may also be very necessary when a certain project chosen can eventually unfold into being more than the individual is capable of handling. Therefore any added support that can be garnered will be very helpful indeed and the individual will not have to deal with the feelings of being overwhelmed.

Having the option of seeking support when needed also encourages those who lend the support to be able to bring a positive element into the otherwise slowly growing stressful situations. The support given, maybe physical or mental, both of which can help to foster positive elements. These elements maybe lacking at a particular juncture of the project, thus the support can fill this need.

Chapter 10:

How Procrastination Can Be A Downward Spiral

Synopsis

Procrastination can lead to a downward spiral. Here are some ways to avoid this destructive behavior pattern and also some recommendations to help overcome an already procrastinating mindset.

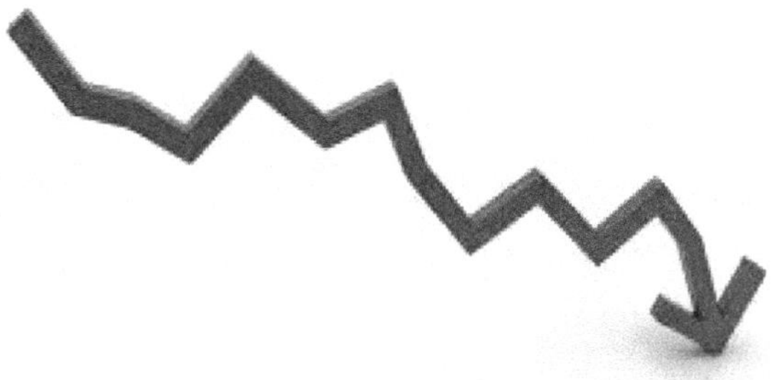

You Ought To Know

Starting a daily simple and non demanding set of tasks list would allow the individual to venture into getting accustomed to a routine and being focused on completing the items on the list within the time frame allotted. In taking this first small step the individual is able to experience the satisfaction derived from the exercise of committing to completing tasks.

Without the practiced and sometimes forced ability to focus and start a task immediately, procrastination gains a foot hold into the situation. Thus by forcing one's self to begin and complete a task this negative element can be kept in check.

Sticking to tasks that can be immediately and easily done is one way to start the individual on actually achieving things on a daily basis. Learning to say "no" to a lot of things, and filtering only those that are immediately workable, will encourage the procrastinating nature to be abandoned.

Playing the waiting game is also another element that should be eliminated in the quest to avoid procrastination. Sometimes people develop the mind set of "ifs", this causes them to wait around until a particular condition or scenario is evident before they are willing to act. This form of procrastination will eventually lead to a lot of lost time and effort on the part of other who are more than willing to get the project started.

Wrapping Up

People who make it a habit of putting off things, end up never getting anything done. If left unchecked this habit can snowball and cause irreparable damage to the individual and those around. Vocalizing the intention of doing something and actually doing it are two very different scenarios, thus procrastination is indeed quite a destructive character trait. Get motivated.

www.ingramcontent.com/pod-product-compliance
Lightning Source LLC
LaVergne TN
LVHW050508210726
843509LV00015BA/3055